TO:

FROM:

D1639144

live, love,
laugh

WRITTEN AND COMPILED BY
AMBER TUNNELL

PETER PAUPER PRESS, INC.
White Plains, New York

*For my friends and family, who have helped me
live brilliantly, love deeply, and laugh always*

Designed by La Shae V. Ortiz

Copyright © 2014

Peter Pauper Press, Inc.

202 Mamaroneck Avenue

White Plains, NY 10601

ISBN 978-1-4413-1414-7

Printed in China

7 6 5 4 3 2 1

Visit us at www.peterpauper.com

live, love, laugh

INTRODUCTION

Who doesn't want a life filled with love, laughter, and gusto—a blockbuster of a life? And yet somehow the challenges and chores of living so often intrude, rewriting the script into a play no one would pay to see. And so the days roll on into weeks and months, and with each pass around the sun we fail to grasp the carousel's gold ring yet again.

But what if we could fully embrace the simple fact that every single day is one we will never get back? "Life changes in the instant. The ordinary instant," says Joan Didion in *The Year of Magical Thinking*. The present moment is the narrow stage on which we live our entire lives. And in all the moments that make up each remarkable and precious day, anything is possible.

"We are made of starstuff. The nitrogen in our DNA, the calcium in our teeth, the iron in our blood, the carbon in our apple pies were made in the interiors of collapsing stars." If we are glorious animations of cosmic ingredients, as Carl Sagan's quote suggests, then who are we not to live fabulous, fun lives filled with epic love?

This modest manifesto, teeming with wisdom from an array of noteworthy icons—from J. R. R. Tolkien to J. K. Rowling, and from Stephen Hawking to Steve Jobs—encourages us along the high road to happiness.

Take heart! Stay curious. Smile often. Swing high. Be foolish. Hug liberally. Dream big. Sing loudly. **LIVE** passionately. **LOVE** deeply. **LAUGH** freely. We are starstuff, and we have the right to shine.

To live is to change, to acquire the words of a story.

BARBARA KINGSOLVER,
The Poisonwood Bible

Anything less than mad, passionate, extraordinary love is a waste of your time.

TIFFANIE DEBARTOLO

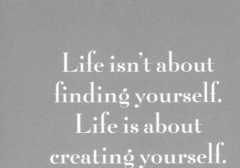

Life isn't about
finding yourself.
Life is about
creating yourself.

GEORGE BERNARD SHAW

We all have the
extraordinary coded
within us,
waiting to be released.

JEAN HOUSTON

We should consider every day
lost on which we have not
danced at least once.
And we should call every
truth false which was not
accompanied by at least
one laugh.

FRIEDRICH NIETZSCHE,
Thus Spoke Zarathustra

You know you're in
love when you can't fall
asleep because reality is
finally better than
your dreams.

DR. SEUSS

The only people for me
are the mad ones,
the ones who are mad to live,
mad to talk, mad to be saved,
desirous of everything
at the same time,
the ones who never yawn or

say a commonplace thing,
but burn, burn, burn like
fabulous yellow roman
candles exploding like
spiders across the stars...

JACK KEROUAC,
On the Road

You will never be
happy if you continue
to search for what
happiness consists of.
You will never live if
you are looking for the
meaning of life.

ALBERT CAMUS

A laugh is a great
natural stimulator,
a pushful entry
into life; and once
we can laugh,
we can live.

SEÁN O'CASEY

Develop your own compass, and trust it. Take risks, dare to fail. … Rehearsal's over.

AARON SORKIN

To live is to be musical,
starting with the blood
dancing in your veins.
Everything living has a
rhythm. Do you feel
your music?

MICHAEL JACKSON

Never love anyone
who treats you like
you're ordinary.

OSCAR WILDE

Stuff your eyes
with wonder, live as if you'd
drop dead in ten seconds.
See the world.
It's more fantastic than
any dream made or paid
for in factories.

RAY BRADBURY,
Fahrenheit 451

At the height of laughter, the universe is flung into a kaleidoscope of new possibilities.

JEAN HOUSTON

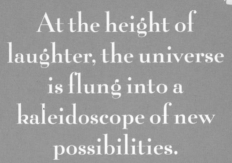

No single event can awaken within us a stranger totally unknown to us. To live is to be slowly born.

ANTOINE DE SAINT-EXUPÉRY

You have to be
unique, and different,
and shine in
your own way.

LADY GAGA

Laughter is poison to fear.

GEORGE R. R. MARTIN,
A Game of Thrones

If you're offered a
seat on a rocket ship,
don't ask what seat!
Just get on.

ERIC SCHMIDT

But I believe in love, you know;
love is a uniquely portable
magic. I don't think it's in the
stars, but I do believe that
blood calls to blood and
mind calls to mind and
heart to heart.

STEPHEN KING,

11/22/63

Your time is limited, so don't waste it living someone else's life. Don't be trapped by dogma—which is living with the results of other people's thinking. Don't let the noise of others' opinions drown out your own inner voice.

And most important,
have the courage to follow your
heart and intuition.
They somehow already know
what you truly want
to become.

STEVE JOBS

Live in the sunshine,
swim the sea,
drink the wild air.

RALPH WALDO EMERSON

All you need is love.
But a little chocolate now
and then doesn't hurt.

CHARLES M. SCHULZ,
"PEANUTS"

To live fully is to let go
and die with each
passing moment, and to
be reborn in each
new one.

JACK KORNFIELD

I don't want to live,
I want to love first and
live incidentally.

ZELDA FITZGERALD

We must laugh and cry,
enjoy and suffer,
in a word, vibrate to our
full capacity....
I think that's what being
really human means.

GUSTAVE FLAUBERT

It does not do
to dwell on dreams and
forget to live.

J. K. ROWLING,

Harry Potter and the Philosopher's Stone

Remember, remember,
this is now, and now, and now.
Live it, feel it, cling to it.
I want to become acutely aware
of all I've taken for granted.

SYLVIA PLATH

To laugh is to live profoundly.

MILAN KUNDERA,
The Book of Laughter and Forgetting

Magic exists.
Who can doubt it, when there
are rainbows and wildflowers,
the music of the wind and the
silence of the stars? Anyone
who has loved has been
touched by magic. It is such
a simple and such an
extraordinary part of
the lives we live.

NORA ROBERTS

It's a crazy world out there. Be curious.

STEPHEN HAWKING

Life's a choice:
you can live in
black and white, or
you can live in color.

KAREN MARIE MONING

Humor keeps us alive.
Humor and food.
Don't forget food.
You can go a week
without laughing.

JOSS WHEDON

If more of us valued food
and cheer and song above
hoarded gold, it would be
a merrier world.

J. R. R. TOLKIEN,
The Hobbit

Life is a fairy tale.
Live it with wonder
and amazement.

WELWYN WILTON KATZ

Love takes off the masks that we fear we cannot live without and know we cannot live within.

JAMES BALDWIN

Don't ask what the world needs. Ask what makes you come alive, and go do it. Because what the world needs is people who have come alive.

HOWARD THURMAN

There is nothing more truly artistic than to love people.

VINCENT VAN GOGH

So many people along the way . . .
will tell you it can't be done.
But all it takes is imagination.
You dream. You plan. You reach.
There will be mistakes.
But with hard work, with belief,
with confidence and trust in
yourself and those around you,
there are no limits.

MICHAEL PHELPS

We loved with a love that was more than love.

EDGAR ALLAN POE

Laughter is timeless.
Imagination has no age.
And dreams are forever.

WALT DISNEY

What sunshine is to flowers,
smiles are to humanity.
These are but trifles,
to be sure; but scattered
along life's pathway, the good
they do is inconceivable.

JOSEPH ADDISON

There is nothing more
beautiful than seeing a
person being themselves.
Imagine going through
your day being
unapologetically you.

STEVE MARABOLI

The law of levity is
allowed to supersede
the law of gravity.

R. A. LAFFERTY

Do not read, as children do, to amuse yourself, or like the ambitious, for the purpose of instruction. No, read in order to live.

GUSTAVE FLAUBERT

Love is the ability to make the invisible visible and the desire always to feel the invisible in one's midst.

ORHAN PAMUK,
My Name is Red

Forget expectations, skip formalities, and live the life you envision. You can't please everyone, but you can always please yourself.

ELIZABETH LEGAN

I like nonsense,
it wakes up the brain cells.
Fantasy is a necessary
ingredient in living. It's a way
of looking at life through the
wrong end of a telescope, which
is what I do, and that enables
you to laugh at life's realities.

DR. SEUSS

For small creatures
such as we the vastness
is bearable only
through love.

CARL SAGAN

LAUGHTER, n.:

An interior convulsion, producing a distortion of the features and accompanied by inarticulate noises. It is infectious and, though intermittent, incurable.

AMBROSE BIERCE,
The Devil's Dictionary

Find your passion and
follow it. . . . Your passion must
come from the things that fill
you from the inside. It will be
grounded in people,
in the relationships you have
with people.

RANDY PAUSCH

It is possible to suffer
and despair an entire
lifetime and still not
give up the art of
laughter.

MADELEINE L'ENGLE

If you are always
trying to be normal,
you will never know
how amazing you can be.

MAYA ANGELOU

Love is a canvas
furnished by nature
and embroidered by
imagination.

VOLTAIRE

Develop an interest in life as you see it; the people, things, literature, music—the world is so rich, simply throbbing with rich treasures, beautiful souls, and interesting people. Forget yourself.

HENRY MILLER

Some people care
too much. I think it's
called love.

A. A. MILNE,
Winnie-the-Pooh

Dwell on the beauty of life.
Watch the stars, and see
yourself running with them.

MARCUS AURELIUS

Laughs are exactly as
honorable as tears. . . .
I myself prefer to laugh,
since there
is less cleaning up
to do afterward.

KURT VONNEGUT

Happiness is a risk. If you're not a little scared, then you're not doing it right.

SARAH ADDISON ALLEN

Common sense and a sense of humor are the same thing, moving at different speeds. A sense of humor is just common sense, dancing.

CLIVE JAMES

Be bold.
If you're going to make an
error, make a doozy, and
don't be afraid to hit the ball.

BILLIE JEAN KING

Live like you are
extraordinary.
Love like you admire
someone's most painful
burden.
Breathe like the air is scented
with lavender and fire.
See like the droplets of rain are

each exquisite.
Laugh like the events of
existence are to be cherished.
Imagine like there is magic
in your fingertips.
Give freedom to your instincts,
to your spirit, to your longing.

E. M. CRANE

From my point of view,
which is that of a storyteller,
I see your life as already
artful, waiting, just waiting
and ready for you to
make it art.

TONI MORRISON

The love for all
living creatures is
the most noble
attribute of man.

CHARLES DARWIN

Vital lives are about action. You can't feel warmth unless you create it, can't feel delight until you play, can't know serendipity unless you risk.

JOAN ERICKSON

When we love, we
always strive to become
better than we are.
When we strive to
become better than we are,
everything around us
becomes better too.

PAULO COELHO,
The Alchemist

My art and
profession is
to live.

MICHEL DE MONTAIGNE

If you can love someone
with your whole heart,
even one person, then there's
salvation in life.

HARUKI MURAKAMI

Laughter is a form of
internal jogging. It moves
your internal organs around.
It enhances respiration.
It is an igniter of
great expectations.

NORMAN COUSINS

Heroes—in myth,
literature, and real life—
take journeys,
confront dragons, and
discover the treasure of
their true selves.

CAROL S. PEARSON

When we are motivated by goals that have deep meaning, by dreams that need completion, by pure love that needs expressing, then we truly live life.

GREG ANDERSON

There is always some madness in love. But there is also always some reason in madness.

FRIEDRICH NIETZSCHE,
Thus Spoke Zarathustra

Life is about not knowing,
having to change, taking the
moment and making the best
of it, without knowing what's
going to happen next.
Delicious ambiguity.

GILDA RADNER

It matters not who you
love, where you love,
why you love, when you
love, or how you love.
It matters only
that you love.

JOHN LENNON

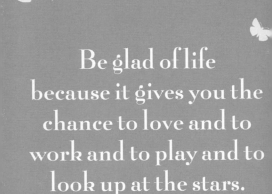

Be glad of life
because it gives you the
chance to love and to
work and to play and to
look up at the stars.

HENRY VAN DYKE

The world is indeed full of peril and in it there are many dark places. But still there is much that is fair. And though in all lands, love is now mingled with grief, it still grows, perhaps, the greater.

J. R. R. TOLKIEN,
The Lord of the Rings

Accept no one's
definition of your life;
define yourself.

HARVEY FIERSTEIN

Our truest response to the irrationality of the world is to paint or sing or write, for only in such response do we find truth.

MADELEINE L'ENGLE

Humor is something
that thrives between man's
aspirations and his limitations.
There is more logic in humor
than in anything else. Because,
you see, humor is truth.

VICTOR BORGE

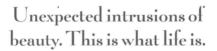

Unexpected intrusions of
beauty. This is what life is.

SAUL BELLOW,

Herzog

I would rather be ashes
than dust! I would rather that
my spark should burn out in a
brilliant blaze than it should be
stifled by dry-rot. I would
rather be a superb meteor,
every atom of me in

magnificent glow, than a
sleepy and permanent planet.
The proper function of man is to
live, not to exist. I shall not waste
my days in trying to prolong
them. I shall use my time.

JACK LONDON

Love is many things,
none of them logical.

WILLIAM GOLDMAN,

The Princess Bride

Great heroes need great
sorrows and burdens,
or half their greatness
goes unnoticed.

PETER S. BEAGLE,
The Last Unicorn

The hardest thing in this world is to live in it. Be brave. Live.

JOSS WHEDON,

Buffy the Vampire Slayer

Go and make interesting mistakes, make amazing mistakes, make glorious and fantastic mistakes. Break rules. Leave the world more interesting for your being here. Make good art.

NEIL GAIMAN

Follow your inner
moonlight; don't hide
the madness.

ALLEN GINSBERG